MELVIL AND DEWEY
IN THE CHIPS

D1564328

MELVIL AND DEWEY IN THE CHIPS

by
Pamela Curtis Swallow

Illustrated by Judith Schroeder

LIBRARIES UNLIMITED
U N L I M I T E D
A Member of the Greenwood Publishing Group

Westport, Connecticut • London

To my family,

the Garden State Writers,

Pat Giff,

and to everyone at Moss School,

especially Melvil and Dewey

Library of Congress Cataloging-in-Publication Data

Swallow, Pamela Curtis.
  Melvil and Dewey in the chips / Pamela Curtis Swallow ; illustrated by Judith Schroeder.
    p. cm.
Summary: Gerbil brothers, Melvil and Dewey, live comfortably in their cage in a school
  library until the day Dewey devises a plan to "bust out."
    ISBN 1-59158-150-8 (pbk. : alk. paper)
    [1. Gerbils—Fiction. 2. Brothers—Fiction.] I. Schroeder, Judith, 1962- ill. II. Title.
    PZ7.S969895Md   2004
    [Fic]—dc22   2004048463

British Library Cataloguing in Publication Data is available.

Library of Congress Catalog Card Number: 2004048463
ISBN: 1-59158-179-6 (set)
          1-59158-150-8 (Melvil and Dewey in the Chips)
          1-59158-151-6 (Melvil and Dewey in the Fast Lane)
          1-59158-153-2 (Melvil and Dewey Gone Fishin')
          1-59158-152-4 (Melvil and Dewey Teach Literacy)

First published in 1986

Libraries Unlimited, 88 Post Road West, Westport, CT 06881
A Member of the Greenwood Publishing Group, Inc.
www.lu.com

Printed in the United States of America

The paper used in this book complies with the
Permanent Paper Standard issued by the National
Information Standards Organization (Z39.48–1984).

10   9   8   7   6   5   4   3   2

CONTENTS

Chapter One
THE PLAN

Dewey stirred and blinked at the morning sun which streaked through cracks in the library window blinds. His gerbil cage was snug and smelled sweetly of cedar shavings. Cuddled next to him was his brother, Melvil, with his furry face tucked tightly under his tail.

Dewey gazed around the large room at the rows and rows of children's books lining the walls. He and Melvil had listened to many stories of adventure being read by Mrs. Alden, the school librarian.

"We *never* go anywhere," muttered Dewey. "It's time we did something about that."

Melvil snorted in his sleep.

The library was a cheery place. Mobiles turned slowly overhead, dangling such phrases as "Keep on Booking." A ceiling pipe was painted to look like a book-worm. Puppets and soft toys sat on shelves. Murals and posters of storybook characters smiled down from the bright yellow walls.

One of Melvil and Dewey's favorite things was a bathtub set in a far corner. This tub had once been in someone's bathroom, but had been discarded and left on a curb. Mrs. Alden had spotted it and convinced Mr. Flynn, the custodian, to bring it into the library and paint it orange. It was filled with comfortable cushions and was a favorite place for children to read and relax. They fought for their turn to be in it. Sometimes Dewey wished he could snuggle in there, instead of being locked in his cage.

Not far from Melvil and Dewey's cage, on the same low counter which stretched below the wall of windows, was a computer. It fascinated Dewey. He watched the children, the teachers, and Mrs. Alden using it, and he paid close attention.

"I want a turn on that," said Dewey. "I want to make that screen light up with colors, music, and beeps. Melvil, are you awake?" Dewey poked Melvil's side and repeated his question.

Melvil mumbled, "Mmmm—huh?"

"I'm bored," complained Dewey.

"Too early. Shhh." Melvil remained curled in his wood-chip nest.

Not discouraged, Dewey continued, "If we could just get out of this cage, we could pick a time when no one would bother us, and we could climb up on the computer and . . ." Dewey grew excited as he planned. He began to bounce lightly on his paws and speak very fast.

"Then we could try it out. I really think we should know about computers, don't you? It's the computer age, Melvil." He gave Melvil another poke.

Dewey's thoughts were interrupted by the sound of Mrs. Alden coming in the door. The lights flickered on, and the librarian, carrying a heavy tote bag, walked into the room. She was followed by two children. Mrs. Alden set down her load and pulled open the window blinds, letting in a shock of light.

"Hi guys," she said as she swept by them into her office at one end of the library.

"What were you saying?" Melvil asked, stretching to his full length and yawning widely. But before Dewey could reply, someone grabbed him by the tail. There he was, dangling over the cage. Melvil was lucky. His handler scooped him up confidently.

"Which gerbil is which?" asked the child now squeezing Dewey.

"I have Melvil. He's the fat one who's always sleeping. You have Dewey. He's the one who's always busy," said the second child.

"Oh, hi Dewey!" said the squeezer. Annoyed, Dewey stared back. The bell rang. The shrieking children dropped the gerbils and ran.

"I really hate that," Dewey said. "Sweaty little hands grabbing me, dangling me. Giggly voices, hot breath."

Melvil was already munching sunflower seeds.

"Listen! I have a plan," Dewey started, but someone was rapping on the cage.

"Hi, little fellas. How ya doing today?" Mr. Flynn asked. He rapped once more with his knuckle before walking off.

"That's another thing that annoys me," complained Dewey. "It gives me a headache and makes me dizzy."

"Boy, these crunchy corn snacks are great," commented Melvil. "Did you try any yet?"

After several more minutes of Dewey's grumbling and Melvil's crunching, the first class of the day filed in. Dewey kept on discussing his plan, in a whisper, but Melvil hushed him so he could hear the fairy tale Mrs. Alden was reading. Dewey eyed the child who sat comfortably in the bathtub during the story. "It isn't fair," he muttered.

As the morning passed, other classes visited. Melvil and Dewey were picked up, tickled, kissed, and squeezed. Even teachers stopped by the cage.

After lunch, several children dashed into the library on their way to class. They dropped leftovers into the

cage, even though they knew they weren't supposed to. A chunk of apple and the corner of an oatmeal cookie landed on Dewey.

Everyone in the school read quietly for fifteen minutes after lunch. Mr. Newman, the principal, stopped in to choose a book. He picked one of the new computer books and sat by the gerbil cage.

"I could really get into that," whispered Dewey, as he saw a picture of a computer screen showing a rocket blasting into space. "Ooh. Think of the beeps and bangs that would make!"

When the silent reading period was over, Mr. Newman put away his book and lifted the top of the cage. Gently, he picked up Melvil and stroked him on the back, then set him down and closed the cage top. "Bye," he called to Mrs. Alden, who was still reading at her office desk.

At last they were alone.

"Melvil, I'm going to leave this place."

"Oh-h-h no. Why?"

"Every day we wake up in this same small cage, in this same small library. Every day we are disturbed from our naps, picked up by our tails, dropped onto our exercise wheel, tickled, annoyed—"

"It isn't so bad, Dewey. We're part of this school. Everyone likes us, visits us, feeds us, holds us—even if they are a bit rough sometimes. It's nice. We're cared for, Dewey."

"But they can come and go. They can sit in the reading tub. They can use the computer. I want to do those things too."

Melvil was silent. Dewey made him nervous.

"Let's bust out of here tonight!" Dewey bellowed.

"I like it here. What if something goes wrong? What if we can't get back into our cage?" said Melvil, as he twisted the end of his tail in his paws.

"Melvil, you worry too much. What goes out, can come in again."

"No. I can't think about this now." Melvil began to burrow under the wood chips. Very soon, there was nothing left for Dewey to talk to but a slowly heaving mound of chips.

Dewey spent the rest of the day and night running on the exercise wheel, digging at the sides of the cage, and thinking of the adventures he could be having outside. Finally, he could no longer contain himself. "I'm going to do it, even if I have to do it alone!" he shouted into the night.

Chapter Two
THE VISITORS

Melvil slept later than usual the next morning. "He's trying to avoid me," grumbled Dewey. Even the sounds of Mrs. Alden readying the library for another day did not wake him. It wasn't until Mr. Flynn came in to talk with Mrs. Alden that Melvil uncurled and squinted at the light.

"Do you want the furniture moved?" asked the custodian. "Who's this guy you've got coming?"

"He's a wildlife expert. The kids should love it."

"Hurray!" squeaked Dewey. "Excitement!"

Before long, carrying cases arrived. Melvil and Dewey strained to catch a glimpse inside but could see nothing through the tiny air vents.

Soon the classes filed in and the program started. While the wildlife expert talked, Dewey began to pace back and forth. "Come on, come on. Let's see some action," he mumbled under his breath.

Then a lock snapped. A latch creaked. Suddenly something flew to the back of a folding chair. Melvil and Dewey stared at the unusual visitor. It was very large, with enormous wings, sharp claws, and a cruel, pointy beak. It turned its gaze toward them. Its eyes met theirs and locked.

"What does he eat?" someone asked.

"He feeds on smaller animals such as rodents," answered the expert.

"Are we rodents?" Melvil asked.

"Don't be silly," Dewey said. "We're gerbils."

Then a loud flap of wings startled everyone in the room. Suddenly the thing was on top of them, gripping the cover of their cage. The gerbils clung to each other, their sides throbbing, as the hungry, piercing eyes stared down at them.

"Don't worry, Ma'am. Everything's under control," said the wildlife man. "I'll just hook this lead to the hawk's leg to keep him over on that chair. No harm done." Looking down into the gerbil cage, he said, chuckling, "Relax fellas, false alarm."

"Perhaps I should move these gerbils," suggested Mrs. Alden.

"No need," the naturalist assured her, as he walked across the library with the bird perched on his arm.

Neither gerbil could speak for a few minutes. After a while Melvil whispered, "I *thought* gerbils might be rodents—you don't know everything, Dewey."

"Let's hide," Dewey said.

"Hide? Where? Our cage is sitting out in the open!" wailed Melvil, crouching as low as he could.

"Burrow into the chips. Come on, dig!" Almost immediately all that could be seen was a quivering mound. They huddled for what seemed like a very long time, hearing only muffled talk and the thumping of their own hearts.

Then it happened. The cage moved. It shook. The top rattled. "Oh-h-h no!" Melvil screamed. "What now?"

"Shhh. Don't move." The cage was jarred again. It sounded as if the top were being knocked off.

CRASH! The top hit the counter.

Trembling under their mound, both gerbils held their breath. Something scooped at their wood chips. The exercise wheel banged the side of the cage. A claw swiped across Melvil's back.

"Grab it! Hurry!" screamed several children.

Digging furiously, both gerbils tried to get lower. Dewey was caught! He shrieked. Melvil tried to hang onto Dewey's front legs.

"No you don't, you rascal," said the wildlife expert, snapping up the weasel that hung over the cage. Dewey was dropped. "At ease, gerbils. Another false alarm."

Mrs. Alden rushed to the cage, glanced in quickly to be sure that Melvil and Dewey were all right, glared at the man and said sharply, "I'm going to move these gerbils to a safe spot. I should have done it before."

In the safety of Mrs. Alden's tightly locked office, Melvil and Dewey began to stir. "I can't believe that happened. One more second and you'd have been that weasel's lunch."

"I know," mumbled a stunned Dewey.

"That weasel meant business!" Melvil said.

"I know."

"What happened to the regular programs—the authors, the illustrators, the puppeteers?" asked Melvil. "They were great, they were fun, they were *safe!*"

"I know."

"Dewey, are you all right?"

Dewey stared blankly into space. The brothers sat side by side, not daring to believe the danger was over. There was no telling what other animal would be let loose.

They ached from sitting so still. Occasionally they heard the children outside the door asking if they could go in and check on the gerbils. At last the door opened.

"I'm sorry, guys," Mrs. Alden said. "It's safe now. I'll move you back where you belong." She lifted the cage, carried it back into the library, and placed it on the counter. She closed the window blinds, picked up her book bag, turned out the lights, and called good-bye to Mr. Flynn as she left.

"This has been the worst day of my life," Dewey sighed.

"I'm too exhausted to talk about it," Melvil answered.

"Well, we've got to talk about it. This was the last straw. I've had it," said Dewey.

But Melvil was already asleep.

How can he sleep at a time like this? Dewey thought. I've got to get through to him before it's too late.

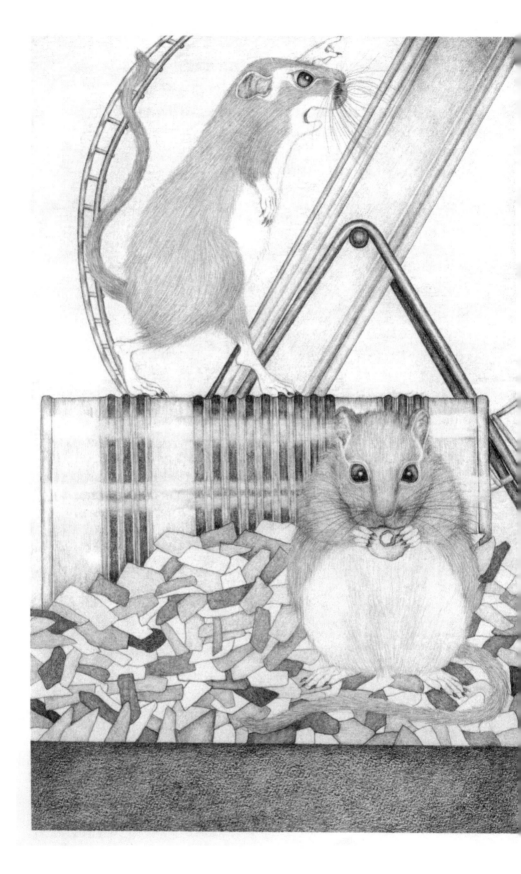

Chapter Three
BUSTING OUT

Each time Dewey tried to discuss the narrow escape they'd had the day before, Melvil changed the subject.

"We've got to do some serious talking, Melvil."

"Boy, this is tasty cereal," replied Melvil, sitting back on his little haunches and holding a piece in his front paws.

"We nearly got killed and all you can talk about is cereal?" snapped Dewey. "Things have gotten out of hand. Face it." Dewey paced back and forth, waving his paw as he spoke. "Our lives could have ended yesterday before we ever had a chance to see the world, climb the highest mountain, or have our turn on the computer!"

Melvil chewed quietly for a few minutes, then replied, "So who wants to climb the highest mountain?"

"Okay, okay, a turn on the computer, then. Melvil, could you please put that snack down and listen?"

Melvil looked around the room, then said softly, "I really like it here, Dewey. It's a nice home." He paused, then added in a voice so soft Dewey could barely hear,

"Besides, I'm not all that brave." He picked up a peanut and rolled it between his paws.

"You won't have to be brave. We're just going to look around a little, nothing scary or dangerous. Please, Melvil. We need a change. We also need to know how to get out of here if we ever have to. Now, are you ready for my plan?"

Dewey could see that Melvil's heart wasn't in it, so he went on quickly, "I've discovered something wonderful. Watch." Dewey began to dig at one side of the cage. Chips flew in every direction.

"Look!" There was a small trap door on the side of the cage. The cage had always been opened from the top.

"Now look," said Dewey. He poked his nose under the door and pushed it up. "After you, Melvil," he said, sweeping his paw toward the door.

"Me first?" squeaked Melvil, whiskers twitching nervously,

"Yep. Out you go."

"Couldn't you go first? After all, it's your plan, Dewey, and I haven't had a chance to think about this. In fact, now that I do think about it . . ."

"Melvil, get on with it."

Melvil stretched his paw through the opening. He hesitated, then went on. Dewey followed. "Oh, WOW! Isn't this super, Mel?" Dewey's feet skidded as he frisked across the smooth counter. Melvil crouched and watched. "Come on, Mel. It feels wonderful!"

Melvil took a cautious step. "I don't like it at all. I like chips under my paws better."

"Let's move on," said Dewey. "You know, I'll bet we'll find some crumbs."

"Crumbs ?" Melvil's nose began to wiggle.

"Sure. Kids bring food; food makes crumbs. Let's go." Dewey wanted to head right for the computer, but he knew he had to lure Melvil, and food seemed the surest way. Besides, saving the best for last was fun.

Melvil shuddered as he looked over the edge of the counter to the floor far below. "How are we going to get down to get the crumbs ?"

"I have it all worked out," Dewey said. "See that window-blind cord hanging over the counter? We'll just climb down that. It'll be easy. Go to it."

"Go to it?" Melvil asked. "Couldn't you go first this time? I still need a bit more time to think about this whole thing."

"Nope. You go. I'll bring up the rear," Dewey replied, giving Melvil a nudge.

"Will we be able to get back up here again and into our cage? You haven't explained everything completely yet."

Knowing it would not be wise to upset Melvil at this point, Dewey said casually, "No problem. What goes down can come up again. Now go on. Down you go."

Melvil grabbed the cord and swung off. Eyes squeezed shut, he simply dangled, swinging from side to side, until Dewey snapped, "Don't just hang there. Open your eyes and inch down." Melvil looked up.

"*Down*, Melvil," said Dewey sharply.

It was a great relief to Melvil when his hind paws finally touched the floor. Feeling very small, he gazed around the room. The gerbil cage looked high and far away.

Dewey dropped to the floor next to Melvil. "This is it! Come on, Mel. We're off to parts unknown!" Dewey bounced as he spoke.

"I don't like the sound of 'parts unknown,' Dewey." Melvil twisted the end of his tail. "You said we were just going to look around. I don't like it. I don't like it at all."

"Don't get yourself stirred up. I have everything under control. What could possibly go wrong?"

Melvil shivered.

**Chapter Four
A DOG AND
A GURGLER**

"I'm turning back," announced Melvil.

"Turning back? We've only just started. Don't spoil everything."

Melvil looked up at the cage. "Melvil, the crumbs. Come on," said Dewey cheerfully as he scurried to the door. Eyes wide with fear, Melvil followed. They looked out into the long hallway. The only sound they heard was the music from the night custodian's radio, which he carried with him as he moved from room to room cleaning. Melvil and Dewey had never seen this custodian. It was Mr. Flynn who always cleaned the library first thing in the morning when he came early to turn on the boiler.

Dewey nudged Melvil. The two gerbils crept quietly down the long corridor. Melvil kept low and as close to the wall as possible. "I don't see any crumbs," he whispered.

"It won't be long," Dewey answered.

They trudged on, but not a single crumb was in sight. Suddenly Melvil jumped at a snuffling sound. "It's nothing," Dewey assured him. They went on.

"Stop breathing down my back," said Dewey.

"I'm not."

"Don't lie . . . I can feel your hot breath." Dewey turned around and let out a gasp. There, right behind them, a whisker's length away, nose to the floor, was the custodian's fat bulldog.

"Run!" Dewey screamed. They scampered as swiftly as they could, with the dog thundering after them. Running faster than they'd ever moved in their lives, they streaked toward a gap at the bottom of a closed classroom door and dove through the narrow space. Dewey had to give his tail a hard yank; it was caught underneath the dog's large front paw.

"Oh m'gosh! A prickly whisker! A wet, slobbery tongue!" gasped Melvil, panting hard. "You told me this wouldn't be scary."

"How was I supposed to know about that dog?" said Dewey. His chest heaved, and his legs trembled. Above the thumping of their hearts, they heard the snorting and scratching of the dog at the door.

"I thought you had this whole thing planned out. Why didn't you know?" Melvil glared at Dewey.

"Did *you*?"

"No, but I wasn't the big mastermind of this adventure. If you'd listened to me, Dewey, we'd be safe in our cage right now."

"We weren't safe yesterday. Have you forgotten that weasel already?" Dewey answered.

Their pounding hearts began to calm. It was then that they noticed the gurgling sound behind them. Melvil's eyes widened. Not daring to turn around, he whispered, "What's that?"

Dewey was silent, frozen with fear. Slowly Melvil turned, but he could not see who or what was making the noise. "You've done it now, Dewey," he muttered angrily. "We're caught between a dog and a gurgler."

The sniffing, scratching, and gurgling continued. Dewey whispered, "Whatever's in here with us is not getting any closer. Maybe it's in a cage. "They remained still for several more minutes. At last the dog grew quiet and trotted down the hall, his license tags jingling.

"He's given up. Let's make a dash for it," suggested Dewey.

"It might not be safe," Melvil said.

"It might not be safe in here, either. We're not alone," Dewey replied. "We'll go on three. One ... two ..." But the sound of footsteps plodding down the hall toward them cut Dewey short.

Chapter Five
TRAPPED!

The tense gerbils stared at the door, listening to the footsteps. The sound stopped outside the door. Their eyes shifted to the doorknob.

"Jake! What's going on?" The voice came from the other side of the door. Melvil and Dewey heard the jingling of dog tags and the click of toenails on the hard floor growing louder.

Jake sniffed at the door again. "What's the matter?" the voice said. "You hear the fish tank gurgling in there? Come on, we'll go in and turn on the tank light for the night. You'll see that you got all excited for nothin'." The dog began to whine.

The doorknob turned and Dewey squealed, "One, two, three, GO!" Two furry objects flashed out the door, scooted between the custodian's legs, scrambled to make a turn, and tore down the hall. The startled dog took up the chase. His feet slipped and skidded as he ran.

"Get back here, Jake! Come here!" commanded the custodian. "Drat that dog."

The chase was on. Dewey, in the lead, saw an open door and dashed in, with Melvil close behind. The bulldog was right behind Melvil. Dewey scrambled up the sleeve of a brown sweater left hanging over a chair. Melvil whimpered as he clambered up after him. The growling dog grabbed the cuff in his teeth and shook it. Melvil hung on with all his might.

Dewey jumped from the top of the chair to the nearby counter. "Hurry, Mel!" he shrieked, hopping up and down. Melvil struggled upward. The dog shook one shoulder of the sweater off the chair and was just pulling the whole thing to the floor when Melvil leaped across to the counter. The dog was furious. He jumped and barked. His front paws almost touched the counter top.

"Quick, hide," said Dewey. They darted behind a pile of books and papers just as the custodian came through the door. They crouched, trembling.

"Jake, get over here. What are you doing? *Bad* dog!" scolded the custodian. He reached down for the sweater and hung it on the chair. Bending and peering, he walked around the room. Closer and closer he came. Dewey swallowed hard, and Melvil squeezed his eyes shut.

"What were you after, Jake? Must have been awfully small. Probably that mouse we've been trying to catch for days." The dog sniffed and whined. "Come on, Jake. We'll come back and eat our supper later." The sound of footsteps and dog tags left the room and went down the hall.

At last it was quiet. Then Melvil spoke. "I never should have let you talk me into this. What a mess."

"I thought it would be different," Dewey answered. "I really wanted to see the school and . . ."

"At this rate, we'll probably never get back alive," snapped Melvil. "I told you that I wasn't very brave, and look what you've put me through." Melvil glared fiercely at Dewey. "And where are all those crumbs you promised?"

"They must be around here somewhere. We've been too rattled to smell anything."

Dewey sniffed deeply. "I think we're warm, though."

Melvil's nose twitched. "I think you're right . . . finally."

The two brothers crept from behind their hiding place. The room was huge. There were tables and chairs in the middle. A refrigerator, stove, soda machine, and some cabinets stood against one wall. Along another wall was a table with two copy machines on it. A third grade spelling test had been left on one machine. "We Care About Your Kids" was written on a round, blue sticker on the door. Next to Melvil and Dewey on the counter were two computers, a stack of magazines, a pile of papers and books, and an unfinished cup of coffee.

"We're getting very close, Mel. This must be the teachers' room."

Melvil's nose glistened with excitement as they crept along the counter. "Look!" said Melvil, pointing to a cracker box lying on its side between the computers.

"After you," said Dewey, grinning at Melvil, who was quivering with anticipation. Once inside the box, they nibbled happily on the leftover crackers. There weren't many left, however, so in a few minutes they backed out onto the counter.

"I'd like a bit more of something," said Melvil, eyes twinkling. "Let's look around some more. I'll bet the teachers who eat here leave lots of things behind."

"You go on," said Dewey, whose attention was focused on a computer manual lying open on the counter. "I want to look at this."

Melvil moved further down the counter. "Ah ha! Hey, Dewey, I'll be busy here for a while." He had found an unfinished bag of potato chips.

"Uh-huh," mumbled Dewey, staring at a diagram of a computer.

Dewey was suddenly startled by the sound of the custodian calling for his dog. They were coming down the hall. "Mel?" Dewey said softly. "Where are you?" He could hear crunching nearby, but there was no sign of Melvil. A feeling of panic swept over him as the sounds of danger grew closer.

"Melvil! We've got to get out of here! Mel, answer me!" He moved toward the direction of the chewing sound. "Mel!" he cried as loudly as he dared. Dewey's throat tightened with fear.

"I'm in the chips," answered a cheerful Melvil, whose blissful munching had prevented him from hearing Dewey's warning. Dewey ducked behind a computer as the man and dog entered the room. Dewey could hear Melvil chewing. He hoped the custodian, who was whistling as he got his paper bag from the refrigerator, could not.

When the whistling stopped, Dewey listened for the sound of Melvil's crunching. It had stopped too. How was Melvil going to get out of that bag? If he moved, he'd be heard.

Slowly, carefully, Dewey peeked around the computer. He saw the man unhook a ring of keys from his

belt and set them on the table. His back was to the gerbils. He leaned over to pour some milk into a bowl for his dog, then switched on his radio.

Dewey heard a faint crackling sound and saw the potato chip bag quiver ever so slightly. He held his breath. Maybe the radio would drown out Melvil. Time seemed to stop. He and Melvil might never get off that counter.

Then a tail emerged from the bag. Next came Melvil's chubby backside. As Melvil looked around, Dewey caught his eye and gestured for him to make a dash for the computer. Melvil sprinted.

The custodian began to talk to his dog about the scraps which would soon be dropped. Dewey whispered softly to Melvil, "I never thought you'd get out of that bag. How'd you do it so quietly?"

"Very, very slowly. Let's get out of here."

"If we're careful," Dewey said, "we can probably move along the counter and down that same brown sweater while the dog is eating. Let's go."

With Dewey in the lead, they scurried behind the second computer. Then, making certain that the dog was busy eating, they shot behind a pile of math books. Again they took a peek before scampering to a stack of magazines. The next stretch was the longest.

They waited, breathing hard, while the custodian scraped an old container of cheese into Jake's bowl. Melvil and Dewey dashed across the counter, down the sweater, and scrambled out the door. They quickly glanced left and right. The hallway looked the same either way. "Uh-oh," murmured Dewey. "Where's the library?"

Chapter Six
BLOWIE!

"Stay calm, Melvil. We'll try one way, and if it's not right, we'll try the other."

"And in the meantime, Dewey, the dog will finish eating and will be hot on our trail again!"

"Let's go." They ran down the long corridor, slowing down at each doorway, hoping to recognize a bit of their library. No luck. They turned and ran back toward the teachers' room. As they neared the door, they darted past as quickly as possible and flew down the hall. Each doorway was the wrong one.

With panic in his voice, Melvil cried, "We're almost to the end! Where is it? I don't remember turning a corner." They reached the last doorway, peered in, and sighed with relief.

"This library sure looks terrific," said Dewey, gazing around the room.

"Those cedar chips are going to feel so good!" Melvil said with a sigh. "I can't wait. What a night. I didn't think we'd make it back here alive."

"Uh, Melvil, just one last thing."

Melvil stared at the cage far above. A worried look crossed his face, and he cradled his tail between his paws. "You do know how to get back up there, don't you?"

"Sure, but there's one more thing," Dewey said.

"After all you've put me through, there's more?" shouted Melvil. "NO MORE!"

"It'll be really quick, I promise. I would have done it first, but you wanted crumbs. It's close to our cage. We'll hop into our chips when we're done." Dewey's eyes shone brightly.

"One thing at a time. I want to know right now how we're going to get up to our cage." Melvil frantically twisted his tail.

"Calm down. We'll just shinny up the same cord we came down."

"Shinnying down is easier than shinnying up, especially when you're chubby."

"I didn't count on that," Dewey admitted.

"How could you not count on it? I've been chubby for a very long time. You can count on my being that way." Melvil paced, waving his tail at Dewey.

"Just grab the cord and try it. Hurry! I hear the dog coming!" In a flash Melvil was up the cord and onto the counter, with Dewey right behind.

"I don't hear anything," said Melvil, "nothing at all." He listened some more, then scowled at Dewey, who grinned back. "You tricked me."

"Well, you shinnied just fine. Now you know you can. One last thing, now. Come on, Mel."

"Not on your life!"

"Aw, Mel, come on. Just one last thing." They crept along the counter toward a large, gray, rectangular object. "This computer is just like the one I saw in the

manual back in the teachers' room. I think I can turn it on." Dewey walked around to the side of it.

"Oh-h-h, no," Melvil said. "I was just beginning to feel safe. You want to get us in trouble?"

"Trouble? How? Watch this." Dewey jumped with all his might against a switch. It clicked and a sudden flash of lights and sounds dazzled them. Melvil cowered. Dewey waved his paw casually at the screen and said, "Someone left the screen turned on and a CD in."

Melvil looked at Dewey with new respect. "How'd you learn all that?"

"I'm awake a lot more than you are. I see people using this all the time. Did you know computers have chips, too?"

Dewey stepped forward and placed a paw on a button. Letters, drifting in blue, instantly filled the screen. Dewey stepped on more keys, jumping a bit at the explosions and the sight of letters being destroyed on the screen.

"WOW! Try this, Mel," he called out. Melvil just watched. "Come on, this is fun. Mel? Don't you want to try?"

Melvil had turned. There below, growling angrily, was the bulldog. "Dewey! We were followed!" Melvil yanked on Dewey's tail to get his attention.

Dewey turned and stared down at the snarling dog. "I've got it! Help me, Mel. Do what I do." Dewey climbed onto the computer keyboard and began to bounce. Melvil followed. The two jumped as hard and as fast as they could.

POW! * BANG! * POP! * BEEP! * BLOWIE!

The startled dog put his tail between his legs and dashed out the door.

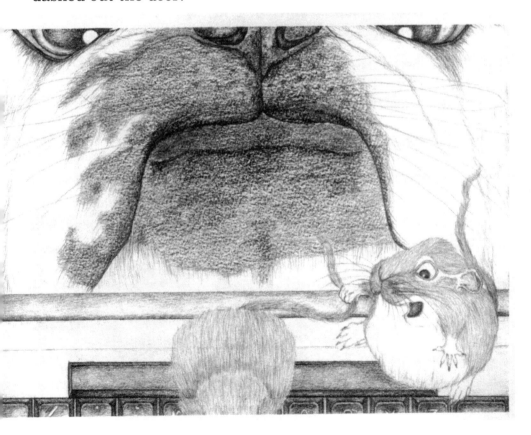

"HURRAY!" cheered Melvil and Dewey, just as a fanfare of music burst forth and a beautiful rainbow-colored balloon rose on the screen. "Ooooooohh," they both exclaimed.

Melvil put a paw on Dewey's shoulder. "What do you say we call it a night, Dewey, before there's more trouble?"

Dewey leaned on the switch and shut the machine off. Side by side the tired brothers made their way along the counter. Dewey began to dig at the side of the cage. "Melvil, you'll have to lean against me. My feet keep skidding out from under."

"There's no chance that we won't get in, is there?" asked Melvil, his nose pressed against the cage.

"We'll get in."

At last the door gave way. "Cage, sweet cage," sighed Melvil as he collapsed into his bowl.

"Are you still angry, Melvil?"

"Well, you could have planned better. But the snacks were good and the computer was great."

"You were brave, Mel. You said you wouldn't be, but you were."

"Do you think so? Maybe I am. Maybe it just doesn't show in a cage," said Melvil thoughtfully.

"It feels good to be back," confessed Dewey. "But it's nice to know we can get out whenever we want." Then he smiled. "Want to try the tub next?"

THE END